RESCUED!

Resting Safely in His Grace

By Christopher Beller

Dedication

THIS BOOK is dedicated to my dad, Paul W. Beller. You left us before I was able to complete this book. You were not able to read it, but I know you are in heaven and understand more about God's grace than I could ever teach or write. Love you, Dad.

Acknowledgments

I WANT TO TAKE A MOMENT to give a few thanks. To my wife, Stephanie, and my three kids: Christian, Jacob, and Azaria. The four of you helped push me to the finish line in writing this book, keeping me on the path even when I thought the path was gone.

To my mother, Virgie. You and Dad raised me to look into the Scriptures, to find the understanding of what God meant in His Word.

And the greatest thanks goes to God, the true author of this book. You have been the inspiration to write this work. To You alone be all the glory.

Contents

Foreword

ONE OF THE STANDOUT QUOTES from Chris Beller's treatment on grace is: "The Pharisee was so focused on how 'good' he was that he missed how full of grace God is." How typical of those who rely on works of the Law rather than on God's grace to focus on the failings of others.

Chris thoughtfully leads us through both the arguments against grace and the arguments for grace. I freely confess that I am one who believes that the arguments for grace are all true and those against, foolish. I am prejudiced. Prejudiced for God's Word.

As we live alongside fellow believers and the lost we should ask ourselves this question: "Do you realize that all the wealth of his extravagant kindness is meant to melt your heart and lead you into repentance?" (Romans 2:4) And another very important verse: "For the grace of God has appeared that offers salvation to all men. It teaches us to say 'No' to ungodliness and worldly passions, and to live self-controlled, upright and godly lives in this present age." (Titus 2:11-12) Both of these verses should open our eyes to the extraordinary power of grace. As we read Chris's narrative and understand the biblical arguments for grace we can share that grace with those around us. Grace provided by the one and only Savior, Jesus Christ.

~ Dan Hefner

✝

I've been waiting for Chris to memorialize the thoughts that have been bouncing around his head for a few years now. Thankfully, this book has captured his love for the true gospel of Jesus Christ. Legalism isn't just for dusty old proponents of the law. It's alive and well in our churches today and if you're not careful, you'll find yourself caught up in this thinking without realizing you're picking up speed on that slippery slope. This book fills a void where a concise and relevant discussion of grace can be accessed without straining through voluminous catalogs of recycled thought. You can carry this with you and dive back in when you need refreshment. Chris, it's about time you wrote this!

~ John Andrews, Author - *The Outlaw Preacher* series

Preface

THIS JOURNEY of my own understanding of grace has been just that, a journey. This journey that has lasted my entire life, and even though I believe I understand it more now than ever, I am still making my way through this incredible trip.

I was born and raised in a godly, Christian home. Both my parents were Christians. My dad's family attended a Methodist church, then became very involved members of a Baptist church. My mom's mother was a combination of Southern Gospel and Pentecostal/Charismatic. Early in my life, while we were members of the previously mentioned Baptist church, my dad came across Kenneth Copeland. We were then introduced to the Word of Faith movement. Kenneth Copeland, Jerry Savelle, Jesse Duplantis, Frederick K.C. Price, among others, became the norm for us, along with the Baptist church.

The Baptist church had "Once Saved, Always Saved" as the foundational salvation doctrine and teaching. I never heard Kenneth Copeland say anything about the concept of losing your salvation other than him saying he never thought about himself losing it. So, growing up, the doctrine I was aligned with was the Baptist point of view.

Before my high school years, we attended a smattering of Baptist and Pentecostal/Charismatic churches. In high school,

I began going to a fundamentalist Baptist Church on my own, and then the last couple of years of high school, we attended a Southern Baptist Church as a family. But even while attending the two churches I never really paid that much attention to the doctrine of salvation. 'Once Saved, Always Saved' was what we, and I, believed.

Fresh out of high school I entered the US military, and began to experience the freedoms of 'being my own man' and the separation from my parents that naturally comes with growing up. I began my time serving in Korea in 1994 as a young man finding his way in the world. Not in God's righteousness, but rather, the darkness of man's sin. I will not go into the details (perhaps that is for another time, another place, and another book), but I do remember feeling that I needed a Bible. Growing up, my dad seemed to have a Bible in every room of the house, but for some reason, I didn't even have one for my one room at the barracks. I went to the small store on the base to look at Bibles. I was looking for a Bible, just a simple KJV Bible to appease my guilty feelings of not having one sitting somewhere in my room. I found one, but it was quite expensive—it was a Scofield Study Bible—and after about two weeks of going back to the store practically every day to look at it, I finally bought it.

After I bought it, it just sat on my desk, untouched and definitely unread. After a month or so, on a Saturday afternoon, bored and with not much to do, and coming off a night of drinking "down range" (the small villages outside of the military bases, or camps), I noticed that Bible sitting there. I picked it up and started reading different passages. I came across Revelation 20:11-15. The Great White Throne Judgment. This passage ends with the words: (verse 15) *And anyone not found written in the Book of Life was cast into the lake of fire.* I set that Bible down, and realized a very sobering thought. If I died that moment, that was where I would go. The Lake of Fire would be my eternal destination.

I believe it was an act of God's grace that brought me to that passage of Scripture. A divine appointment with a God who loved me, even though I had quite a road to travel before I really began to understand what that love and grace truly was and truly meant.

Throughout the years following that event, I grabbed hold of various doctrines and teachings, attended various churches, most of them being of the Pentecostal alignment. My understanding of grace took on a form radically different from my childhood. A lot of this I attribute to separating myself from what my parents, especially my dad, believed in regards to the Salvation Doctrine. Instead of 'Once Saved, Always Saved,' I became steeped in the view that every sin you committed (after 'initial salvation') separated you from God. You then needed to beg for forgiveness, and hopefully, your heart would not be so hardened that He would refuse you your re-entry into His salvation, and once again be saved and born again. And maybe this time, it would stick. I would sin, lose my salvation, then repent to be saved again. What my understanding ultimately came down to was this: I could not save myself, but now that I was saved, I better do everything I could to keep my salvation. In other words, it wasn't God keeping me, it was the strength of my own will.

After years of this destructive cycle, I began to see it a little bit differently. Not much, but a little bit. Instead of *every* sin ending your 'current salvation,' God would keep you, unless you chose to leave His grace. This was my doctrine for several years, but even that understanding kept me in the dark, bound to my own 'good works.' The unanswered question became: at what point does one choose to no longer be saved? What sin was the cutoff, the final point of no return? Both of these doctrinal views injected my own performance into the equation of my salvation, essentially removing God's grace. And my own performance could never and would never be enough to save me, no matter how good and for how long I went without sinning (and believe me, it never really went very long before I would).

Enter into my life first, my close friend and mentor, Dan Hefner (Worship Leader and Bible teacher at a local church), followed by probably the closest friend I have ever had, John Andrews (author of *The Outlaw Preacher* series and Bible teacher/preacher extraordinaire [ha ha]). Both of these men taught a grace that just seemed too good to be true. And so, I held out that we could not necessarily lose our salvation, but we could still 'give it up.' But they persisted, and the cracks began to form.

I began to see things in the Bible I never really noticed before. I began to read verses I never seemed to have read, or that I read over without thinking about what it was I was reading. I remember a conversation I had with John one day in his truck on our way back to the church after placing out signs. "I feel like I am standing on the precipice, looking out over a dark unknown," I began to explain to him. "I am seeing things in Scripture now that I have never seen before, and I know what I have believed for the better part of 20-plus years is not the truth." It was scary to me to stand there looking at what was behind me (false teachings, notions, and understandings), but so exciting to look out into the unknown (what I knew deep inside to be the truth). I told him that "if I take that step, then I am announcing that the majority of what I have believed for so long is false." That is a scary place to be!

John's answer to me? "Just take that leap of faith, bro. He will be there to catch you and carry you into all the Truth there is, and you will begin to experience the greatest ride of your life!"

Well, I took that step, that leap of faith. And here I am still on this journey, still learning about God's grace, what it is and what it means and what it does in the life of a sinner who dares to believe in a God who loves him. And yes, this is the greatest, most exciting ride of my life. I am so thrilled that you have chosen to take a look at this little book and maybe you, too, will join me on this journey. It is a lifelong trip, one filled with wonders and struggles, but also one that will change you from the inside out. Only God's grace can do that, and that truth is what this book is all about. So hold on; this is just the very beginning of this grace trip!

CHAPTER ONE
Grace

WHY does this one, five-letter word bring so much division to The Church? Why are there so many good-intentioned preachers and pastors who seem to view 'grace' as a ploy of Satan, a trap that is only meant to entangle their people in sin? So many times we hear a sermon about sin, wrath, shame, and guilt, and when those sermons are preached, the preacher is praised for being able to hear the voice of the Lord. But when a preacher preaches a message of hope, deliverance, mercy, and grace, that preacher is shouted down and referred to as 'hyper-grace,' a heretic, or sometimes, something much worse.

The New Testament is full of God's mercy. It is full of hope and deliverance. The New Testament is bursting at the seams with God's grace! Yet we are constantly reminded of the wrath of God. We are constantly scolded and, never too gently, to "REPENT! So that you may flee the wrath to come!" Grace seems, too many times, to be an afterthought. Just something to talk about after everyone knows about sin, wrath, shame, and guilt.

I believe that God's view of us, before and after salvation, is not one of wrathful ridicule and angry destruction, but rather, one of kindness, mercy, and a love that goes so much deeper than the deepest depths of human existence. It has to be. For God to reach any sinner (and that includes every single individual who reads this book), his grace had to be deeper than our sin, stronger than our weaknesses, and more lovely than our sinful wretchedness. That is the God who loves. That is the God who IS love. That is the God who, just when you think He could no longer be able to love you any more, He reveals another completely new level of love and grace. The Bible declares this grace to be the central message of Jesus Christ of Nazareth.

In this book, we will be looking at this grace, this incomparable grace that can lift the vilest sinner out of the miry clay. We will be taking a look at God's immeasurable mercy, a mercy that no one ever deserves, no matter how 'good' you think you may be. We will also be looking at this unconquerable love. A love that, even though we experience it, we cannot fathom it, we cannot write down the correct words to describe it.

My hope and prayer is that those who read this book are those who need this book. I believe it is time that God's grace be properly regarded, genuinely reflected, and Biblically revealed. This book is for those who have run from God because of the "wrathful God" that is preached. This book is for those who have given up hope because those "in the faith" denied hope to those who need it most. This book is for the sinner and the saint, the righteous and the unrighteous, and the lost as well as the found. In other words, this book is for every individual on this planet. This message is the Gospel of Jesus Christ. It is time The Church rises up out of the ashes of judgment and condemnation and begins to offer mercy, grace, and hope to a lost world. That is my hope and prayer in writing this book.

CHAPTER TWO
The Gospel of The Grace of God

(ACTS 20:24) *But none of these things move me; nor do I count my life dear to myself, so that I may finish my race with joy, and the ministry which I received from the Lord Jesus, to testify to the gospel of the grace of God.*

These were the words of the Apostle Paul to the Ephesian Church leaders. Isn't it interesting that Paul would say his life was meaningless if he was not testifying of the Gospel of the Grace of God? It is also interesting to me that Paul would go so far as to say it was the ministry given to him from none other than the Lord Jesus. Preaching grace was Paul's life. It is what God called him to do. Do not simply shrug that off. Paul wrote 13 of the 27 books in the New Testament. If this was his life's ministry, and he wrote two-thirds of the New Testament Bible, then I would say the grace message is more than important. But what is this so-called 'grace message'? Paul lays it out for us in 1 Corinthians 15.

(1 Corinthians 15:1-4) *Moreover, brethren, I declare to you the gospel which I preached to you, which also you received and in which you stand, by which also you are saved, if you hold fast that word which I preached to you—unless you believed in vain. For I delivered to you first of all that which I also received: that Christ died for our sins according to the Scriptures, and that He was*

buried, and that He rose again the third day according to the Scriptures.

We keep seeing the word 'gospel.' But what in the world does that word even mean? I am glad you asked! The word 'gospel' simply means 'good news.' When you see written, "The Gospel of Jesus Christ according to the Apostle John," what is really being said is this: "The Good News of Jesus Christ according to the Apostle John". What Jesus offers is *good* news! So why do so many in The Church want to give out bad news? Why do so many churches open their doors on Sunday mornings to condemn those whom God loves?

I have been told that the sinner needs to understand the 'bad news' before they can understand the 'good news.' I can understand that … to a point. Too often we want to focus on nothing but the bad news, and then mention the good news as a footnote to the message. We want to make sure the sinners know fully and completely what awful, despicable creatures they truly are. We feel that it is our job and duty to call down the fire of judgment on those who are lost. And then ... if we have time, say a little something about Jesus' love and sacrifice for them. But listen, Jesus *is* the message, and His message was The Gospel. There is no other message to preach.

(Mark 16:15) *And He said to them, 'Go into all the world and preach the gospel to every creature.'*

Jesus did not say to the disciples to go and make sure everyone knows what awful, horrible, despicable sinners they have been. Sinners knows the despicable and wretched things they have done. They may not admit it, but when they are looking in the mirror at themselves, they know. The sinner does not need us pointing our fingers in his face, shouting him into shame and condemnation. It is not the job of The Church to convict the sinner of his or her sins. Jesus said, in John 3:17, *For God did not send His Son into the world to condemn the world, but that the world through Him might be saved.* If Jesus was not sent into the world to condemn the world, then why do we, as his body, feel it is our job and duty to condemn the world?

His command was to proclaim the Gospel. Go into the world and proclaim the Good News. What is the Good News?

In this world we live in, there seems to be nearly nothing but bad news. You cannot turn on the news or read the paper or visit your favorite news website without seeing, hearing, and reading about bad stuff happening. There almost always seems to be a war going on somewhere. The President messed up this, Congress messed up that. Someone has been murdered. Another has been raped. And another has been robbed. One country is threatening another country while this race or that group of people is being discriminated against. We see it all the time, all day long, day after day, week after week, year after year. I believe it is past time for a change. I believe it is time the world hears some good news. And if The Church is not going to be the one to step up to the plate and tell the world what Jesus has done ... then nobody will.

But again, what is the Good News? What is this 'Gospel of the Grace of God' that the Apostle Paul spoke so highly of that the meaning and purpose for his ministry and life dwelt on it?

(John 3:14-18) *And as Moses lifted up the serpent in the wilderness, even so must the Son of Man be lifted up, that whoever believes in Him should not perish but have eternal life. For God so loved the world that He gave His only begotten Son, that whoever believes in Him should not perish but have everlasting life. For God did not send His Son into the world to condemn the world, but that the world through Him might be saved. He who believes in Him is not condemned; but he who does not believe is condemned already, because he has not believed in the name of the only begotten Son of God.*

Those were the words Jesus spoke to the Pharisee, Nicodemus, in John Chapter 3. In that passage, Jesus said what is probably the most well-known Bible verse in the entire Bible, John 3:16. Most of us know it, or have at least heard it. Even if you have never stepped foot in a church, you most likely have heard someone say it: *For God so loved the world, that he gave his only begotten Son, that whoever believes in Him should not perish but have eternal life.*

That is the Gospel, the Good News, wrapped up in one incredible verse. The Good News is that someone else died in my place. Someone else died in your place. This death was not accidental. He was not murdered. He chose to die, when to die, and how to die. And He did not have to do any of it. He chose it.

A message of love, mercy, hope, and grace because God so loved the world. In John 3:16, Jesus did not say, "For God loved the world *enough* ..." No, He said so very clearly, "For God *so* loved the world ..." God so loved the world. That is the Gospel message. That is the answer to sin. That is the answer to condemnation. That is the message Jesus wants proclaimed to the nations, what He wants proclaimed to the sinner, and what He wants proclaimed to the saint.

We do not need to die in, for, or because of our sins, and we do not need to suffer the penalty for our sinfulness. There is One who was sent and suffered and died in our place. That is the Good News that we, The Church, should be shouting and proclaiming: Jesus *so loved* the world that he died for the world, so that the world could be saved!

There is more to life than waiting to hear the bad news.

There is Good News that Jesus declares to us, and desires to declare through us as The Church, His Body. We are to be the moon to his sun (see Song of Solomon 6:10), reflecting the light of love to a darkened world. But we cannot do that if we are so focused and constantly consumed by condemnation. You simply cannot extend the hand of friendship if your hand is curled into a point of judgment. We have something the world needs, and His Name is Jesus. And in that Name is the consummation of the Gospel of the Grace of God. We, The Church, are His light-bearers, the proclaimers of His Gospel, His Good News!

CHAPTER THREE
But What About Sin?

HAVE YOU EVER heard the phrase, 'a license to sin'? Perhaps you have even said that phrase in response to the message of grace. I know I have heard it too many times to count. It practically never fails: A preacher, a pastor, or an evangelist will preach or teach about God's grace, and someone will speak up with the response that, "If grace is preached, then people will be given a license to sin." The answer I have heard to that criticism was simply, "People don't need a license to sin, they are doing a pretty good job of that without one!"

But what about the abuse of Grace? Of course there are abusers of grace out there. But there are also abusers of water baptism, but does that mean we stop preaching water baptism? No, of course not. We just teach and preach the proper usage of water baptism. What about the Gifts of the Spirit? What about Tongues, specifically? Those of you who are Charismatics and/or Pentecostals, are there abusers of the gift of tongues? Of course there are. In fact, the Apostle Paul addressed some issues when he wrote to the Corinthian church. But does that mean we stop preaching and teaching Tongues and the other Gifts of the Spirit? No, we just simply teach the proper usage of Tongues and the other Gifts of the Spirit. Proper teaching brings proper balance. But why is it that The Church wants to throw the Grace message out because there are abuses of it? What people need is proper teaching and proper preaching: a balanced, Biblical view and understanding of it. The primary issue, I believe, is not truly understanding what Jesus did on the cross regarding sin and the sinner.

(2 Corinthians 5:17-21) *"Therefore, if anyone is in Christ, he is a new creation; old things have passed away; behold, all things have become new. Now all things are of God, who has reconciled us to Himself through Jesus Christ, and has given us the ministry of reconciliation, that is, that God was in Christ reconciling the world to Himself, not imputing their trespasses to them, and has committed to us the word of reconciliation. Now then, we are ambassadors for Christ, as though God were pleading through us: we implore you on Christ's behalf, be reconciled to God. For He made Him who knew no sin to be sin for us, that we might become the righteousness of God in Him."*

This is the passage that the Holy Spirit used to really open my closed mind about God's grace. In this passage, we read, "that is, that God was in Christ reconciling the world to himself, not imputing their trespasses to them, and has committed to us the word of reconciliation."

I'm sure this next statement will upset some people, but I feel it must be said, and must be said before we get farther in this book: The sin problem has been dealt with. Paul wrote as much in 2 Corinthians 5:19, quoted above. He is talking about what Jesus did on The Cross. He mentions that he who is in Christ is a new creation. The only way to be 'in Christ' is through salvation. There is only one way that salvation was made possible: the Cross of Christ. Paul clearly and simply writes that God was reconciling a sinful humanity through Christ, and that He was not counting their trespasses against them. This is the Message of

Reconciliation that Paul is talking about.

In other words, God canceled the debt of sin, a debt we could not pay, through Christ and the Cross. He reconciled the account held against humanity. He paid the eternal bill that was against us and stamped, 'Paid In Full' over it. Don't misunderstand me. I am not talking about Universalism here. Man is still responsible for faith, or the lack thereof. But the issue of sin, as far as God is concerned, is dealt with. When Jesus said, "It is finished," he meant exactly that. He was the One sacrifice for all, once and for all time.

Let me ask you this question, to hopefully help you understand what I am saying. When did the Cross take place? Nearly two thousand years ago. When were you born? On a more personal level, when was the last time you sinned? This morning? Yesterday? This afternoon or evening? Did you ask for forgiveness? Did you beg, plead, and weep, hoping God would hear you? Did Jesus have to climb back up on the cross and sacrifice himself once again for your latest dive into the pool of sin? If Paul said that in Christ God was reconciling the world to Himself and was not holding their trespasses against them, then why are we begging and pleading for God to do something He already said He had done? We thank Him for His forgiveness. You sinning did not throw God into a tailspin, causing Him not to know what to do or how to address your latest slip into sin.

(John 3:18) *He who believes in Him is not condemned; but he who does not believe is condemned already, because he has not believed in the name of the only begotten Son of God.*

These were the words of Jesus to Nicodemus from John Chapter 3. Notice what Jesus says about condemnation. He says "Whoever *does not believe* is condemned already." WHY? Because he has *not believed* in the name of the only Son of God. Jesus did not say, "He who sins is condemned already, because he has sinned once again." The issue is not sin, it is *not believing*.

The Apostle Paul wrote in Romans 14:23, *Whatever does not proceed from faith is sin*. The world faces a 'faith' problem. The world simply does not believe; the world simply does not have faith in Christ Jesus. Too many times we want to point the finger at sin, and condemn because of sin. But what did Jesus say was the reason for the condemnation? It was because of what people do not believe!

Now, what about sin? What about preaching against sin? Do we preach a relaxed view of sin, allowing sin to remain in our lives? What about clean living? Should a Christian continue living in sin once he or she is saved? These are all very important questions, questions that the Apostle Paul addressed in his writings, especially Romans 5-7. But before we get into what Paul said about them, let us first take a look at what Jesus said about remaining in sin.

(John 7:53 – 8:1-11) *And everyone went to his own house. But Jesus went to the Mount of Olives. Now early in the morning He came again into the temple, and all the people came to Him; and He sat down and taught them. Then the scribes and Pharisees brought to Him a woman caught in adultery. And when they had set her in the midst, they said to Him, "Teacher, this woman was caught in adultery, in the very act. Now Moses, in the law, commanded us that such should be stoned. But what do You say?" This they said, testing Him, that they might have something of which to accuse Him. But Jesus stooped down and wrote on the ground with His finger, as though He did not hear. So when they continued asking Him, He raised Himself up and said to them, "He who is without sin among you, let him throw a stone at her first." And again He stooped down and wrote on the ground. Then those who heard it, being convicted by their conscience, went out one by one, beginning with the oldest even to the last. And Jesus was left alone, and the woman standing in the midst. When Jesus had raised Himself up and saw no one but the woman, He said to her, "Woman, where are those accusers of yours? Has no one condemned you?" She said, "No one, Lord." And Jesus said to her, "Neither do I condemn you; go and sin no more."*

Oh, how I wish The Church would listen to the words of Jesus here. What is his reaction to those who were judging the woman? He challenged them, *Let he who is without sin among you cast the first stone.* We love to judge others. We love to point the finger. We love to stand over the sinner and declare loudly our own righteousness. But Jesus says, 'Look at yourself, and if you are without sin, then you can cast that stone of judgment you hold at your fingertips.'

After all the judges left, and no one was left to condemn her, He tells the woman, *Neither do I condemn you ...* But that is not all he says to her. Many times, I hear the argument to excuse sin, and it includes this passage. It is used in a way to allow sin to abound, and for the sinner or Christian to continue in sin. But Jesus did not stop at, *Neither do I condemn you.* He continues with, *Go, and from now on sin no more.* Go and sin no more. That is what Jesus said. He forgives, but He also commands.

What I see, sadly, is that many want Jesus Christ the Savior. The meek and mild Jesus, the One who forgives and heals and blesses. But when it comes time to follow Jesus Christ the Lord, well, that is another story. We don't care much for being told what we need to do or not do. We want to be our own masters, our own lords. We want to set up our own standards and rules and regulations. And usually, those standards, rules, and regulations fall so short of what God has commanded us to do or not do. We love Jesus the Savior. But what about Jesus the Lord?

(1 Corinthians 6:19-20) *Or do you not know that your body is the temple of the Holy Spirit who is in you, whom you have from God, and you are not your own? For you were bought at a price; therefore glorify God in your body and in your spirit, which are God's."* (1 Corinthians 7:23a) *"You were bought at a price ...*

We have been set free, this is true. But what is this freedom? Jesus said in John 8:36, *If the Son has set you free, you will be free indeed.* The Son has, indeed, set us free. He has purchased us; He has paid a high price for us: His Own Blood. We have been redeemed, and we do not belong to ourselves. We belong to Him, the Lord of Glory. We believers, we Christians, are Temples of the Holy Spirit living within us, and we are not to defile this Temple. He has commanded us to walk upright lives and has given us very clear directions on what and what not to do. These are not mere suggestions. They are commands from the One who bought us from the slave markets of sin. We were made free *from* sin, not made free *to* sin.

Throughout the New Testament, we read of what to put away, what to flee from, what to not partake of. As a father, I command my children to not do drugs, to not take part in sexual immorality, to not steal or lie or kill. I command them to not do these things, to be respectful of others, to forgive others of doing wrong to them. Why? Because I know the end result of those things. Our Father, God, also knows the end result of those things. That is why He commands us to not partake of sin. Paul writes in Romans 6:23, *For the wages of sin is death ...* God knows the end result of sinfulness: It is death. But thankfully, Romans 6:23 does not end with that statement. Paul continues to write *... but the free gift of God is eternal life in Christ Jesus our Lord.* We receive the free gift by faith. We believe what God has said is true. And because we believe, we put away sin and walk in righteousness in Him.

In Romans Chapter 5, Paul talks about us having peace with God through faith, and how we suffered death in Adam, but now life in Christ. He talks about how in one man's (Adam's) disobedience, we all were made sinners. We were born with that nature. We were not sinners because we sinned, we sinned because we were sinners. We were born losers. We were born sinners. We were actually stillborn spiritually. We had that nature. That nature was so intricately a part of us, it made up our very being. We had the very stench of sinful death clinging to us, chained to us as the Apostle Paul says in Romans 7. There was nothing we could do about that. We were sinners, simply put. But because of Jesus' death in our place on the Cross, we now can partake of Him by grace, through faith (Ephesians 2:8-9). He became our sin, so that we could become the righteousness of God (2 Corinthians 5:21).

Back to the topic at hand ...

(Romans 5:18-21) *Therefore, as through one man's offense judgment came to all men, resulting in condemnation, even so through one Man's righteous act the free gift came to all men, resulting in justification of life. For as by one man's disobedience many were made sinners, so also by one Man's obedience many will be made righteous. Moreover the law entered that the offense might abound. But where sin abounded, grace abounded much more, so that as sin reigned in death, even so grace might reign through righteousness to eternal life through Jesus Christ our Lord.*

Here Paul states that a Man, Jesus, actually reversed the action of another Man, Adam. Adam's disobedience was reversed by Jesus' obedience. This is a clear fact in the Scriptures. But what about the Christian who still sins? The argument given by some is that where sin increased, grace abounded. That is the Bible, after all, right? The argument I have seen from many so-called 'grace preachers' is this: Go and do what you want (quite opposite from what Jesus said in John Chapter 8, isn't it?). Go and sin, enjoy your life, do whatever you want! Sex, drugs, and rock 'n roll ... because, you know ... grace! Paul addresses this argument also. In fact, he confronts this argument head on, right after the above quoted passage of Romans 5:18-21.

(Romans 6:1-2) *What shall we say then? Shall we continue in sin that grace may abound? Certainly not! How shall we who died to sin live any longer in it?*

How can we who have died to sin still live in it? Good question. Paul compares our relationship to sin as a wife to a dead husband. She is no longer under the marriage vows to the husband. She has been made free from that marriage. We have been made dead to sin; therefore, we are no longer under the bondage to sin. So, don't continue in sin.

A close friend gave this analogy: Imagine a woman is abused by her husband. He physically, verbally, emotionally abuses her, constantly. She divorces the abusive man and marries a good man, one who is always there for her, takes care of her, and provides for her. He loves her to the point of even giving his own life for her. He is everything good to her, and everything good for her. But the abusive ex-husband will still call her for a hook up. She knows who is on the other end of the phone from the Caller ID ... but she still answers and sneaks away to be with the abusive ex-husband for "just one more time" (does that sound familiar?), only to be beaten and abused, left with the wounds and afflictions of her actions. She has the love she needs, the love she craves right there at home in the good husband who loves her, but she continues to return to the rotten abuser. Now tell me, what would you think of her? Thoughts of weakness? Thoughts of ignorance? Thoughts of 'What in the world is wrong with this person?' Am I right? Perhaps you have even been that person who continues to run back to the abusive relationship. I would think we have all been that person when it comes to our relationship with Jesus. At least once in our Christian walk, we have returned to sin, even if for only a brief time. For the abused to continue to return to the abuser is what it is like for the Christians to return to the sin they have been set free from.

(Romans 6:15-23) *What then? Shall we sin because we are not under law but under grace? Certainly not! Do you not know that to whom you present yourselves slaves to obey, you are that one's slaves whom you obey, whether of sin leading to death, or of obedience leading to righteousness? But God be thanked that though you were slaves of sin, yet you obeyed from the heart that form of doctrine to which you were delivered. And having been set free from sin, you became slaves of righteousness. I speak in human terms because of the weakness of your flesh. For just as you presented your members as slaves of uncleanness, and of lawlessness leading to more lawlessness, so now present your members as slaves of righteousness for holiness. For when you were slaves of sin, you were free in regard to righteousness. What fruit did you have then in the things of which you are now ashamed? For the end of those things is death. But now having been set free from sin, and having become slaves of God, you have your fruit to holiness, and the end, everlasting life. For the wages of sin is death, but the gift of God is eternal life in Christ Jesus our Lord.*

The Apostle Paul is very clear. Do not continue in sin. Do not make yourselves slaves once more to sin. Do not let sin reign in your mortal body. Do not let sin have dominion, or rule, over you. We do not belong to ourselves; we belong to the One who purchased us with a price. We are to put to death the deeds of sin and live in righteousness. We have been set free from sin, and are now slaves of righteousness, servants of God. But in that service, instead of eternal death, we have eternal life. So I challenge you as I challenge myself, and as Jesus challenged the woman caught in adultery. In answer to the question, "What about sin?" My answer is this: go and sin no more.

CHAPTER FOUR
Grace, Faith, Works: The Proper Mix

IN THE LAST CHAPTER, we addressed sin and sinfulness in the life of the Christian. First, what God—through Jesus—did concerning sin, and second, a proper view of sin through the lens of grace.

For years, I was taught and believed that even though I could not save myself, it was up to me and all my good works to keep myself saved. I was trapped in a vicious and endless cycle: Sin–> Repent–> Repeat. I would sin, then I would feel so horrible about committing sin, I would repent. Maybe I would be able to go a few hours, perhaps a day ... sometimes even a few days, but eventually, I would slip face-first back into that sin, repeating the whole process over again. Go back to the starting line, start over.

As a child, I remember playing a game with my cousins and my dad: "Father May I?" (The original name I guess was "Mother May I?") The game was played with all of us kids on one side of the room and my Dad on the other. The goal of the game was to reach him before the others would. He would say, for example, "Chris, move two big steps forward." If I asked, "Father May I?" he would say, "Yes, you may," and I would take two big steps towards him. If I did not say those three magic words, I would have to go back to the very beginning and start all over. That's the way the 'Sin–> Repent–> Repeat' cycle plays out. I start out, ready to make it this time, only to falter and not do what I was supposed to do, and have to start all the way back at the beginning! Like I said, a vicious and endless cycle.

We tend to rely too much on our good works. We have this attitude and mindset that it all hangs on us 'crossing our T's and dotting our I's.' In other words, no matter how good we think we are, we miss the target, and we mess it up. We fall into this trap that says, "You cannot save yourself, but you better make sure you keep yourself saved." This trap is so easy to fall into. Why? Because we *want* to do good. Every Christian desires to do what is good all the time. And it is so very easy to slip from a desire to do good works to earning our salvation because of our good works.

Paul wrote in Galatians 1:6-7, *I marvel that you are turning away so soon from Him who called you in the grace of Christ, to a different gospel, which is not another; but there are some who trouble you and want to pervert the gospel of Christ.* You see, Galatians was written to Christians who were turning to another 'gospel,' a gospel mixing works and grace; a 'gospel' that would say you had to be saved by grace, but you then had to keep the Law to stay saved, to keep yourself saved. The Apostle Paul stated there is no other gospel other than the gospel he preached, and if anyone is preaching to you a gospel contrary to the one you received, let him be accursed. (Galatians 1:9) The only gospel there truly is, is the Gospel of the Grace of God. What we need to do is to understand the proper mix of grace, faith, and works. We need to understand what part God plays in the salvation process, and what part we play in the salvation process.

(Ephesians 2:8-10) *For by grace you have been saved through faith, and that not of yourselves; it is the gift of God, not of works, lest anyone should boast. For we are His workmanship, created in Christ Jesus for good works, which God prepared beforehand that we should walk in them.* What we read there in Ephesians 2 is the mixture that is needed, which then brings the end result. God's ingredient is grace. We had to be recipients of His grace. No way could we be accepted other than by His great grace. Absolutely, positively, no other way. You could not, you cannot, and you never will be able to earn your way to the Father.

Isaiah 64:6 tells us, *But we are all like an unclean thing, and all our righteousness are like filthy rags.* The term used there for 'filthy rags' literally means a used menstruation rag, a stained garment. Our very best good works are nothing but contaminated, bloody rags so defiled they have to be burned. Can you imagine standing before God, and saying to Him, "Hey, take a look at how awesome I am!" then you toss a bloody and contaminated rag at the foot of the Throne. "Get a load of that, God! Look at how great I am!"

What would His reaction be? Yet, we do that every time we rely on our own righteousness, our own good works, as though that is good enough to confidently stand before Him. That is why it has to be by His grace. That is why we cannot boast. Our very best deeds are not good enough, and our very best of our best deeds will never be good enough to earn salvation.

It was God's great grace that sent Jesus to this world, to live a life fully pleasing to God, fulfilling the Law, and then offering up His perfection in our place. Only by grace could we be saved. That grace was God's part in the mixture. And let me tell you this ... His grace was the majority ingredient. His gift was the dominant ingredient in this sweet mixture we call salvation.

But for all of God's grace, we still have a part in the process. Again, look at Ephesians 2:8, "... through faith." You have to believe. We have to believe, we have to believe to receive the grace that God offers. We have to believe that God so loved the world that He gave His Son (John 3:16). We have to believe that God's love was so great that His Son shed His blood and died in my place, and that He died in your place. We have to believe that God's grace, His favor that we did not earn, that we could not earn, and that we could or would ever deserve, was given to us. It is *by* grace, *through* faith. No matter how much God loves you, you still have to believe. No matter how much suffering Jesus went through on your behalf, you still must believe. We have to believe that Jesus is enough, and what He accomplished on the cross is enough, that His blood that was shed is enough. It must be through simple faith.

But what about the good works? Does that mean we can just coast through our lives and never do anything good? After all, good works will not save us, right? Read on in Ephesians 2: *For we are His workmanship, created in Christ Jesus for good works, which God prepared beforehand, that we should walk in them.*

The word used for 'workmanship' means 'a thing that has been made.' The Bible declares in Psalms 139:14 that we "are fearfully and wonderfully made." In other words, we are God's masterpieces. We are works of art, created by God. And we now, as believers, have been recreated in Christ Jesus. 2 Corinthians 5:17 states, *Therefore, if anyone is in Christ, he is a new creation; old things have passed away; behold, all things have become new.* The Bible also declares in Colossians 3:3, *For you died, and your life is hidden with Christ in God.*

You and I are works of art, created by the very hands of God, in Christ. So much so that our very lives are hidden in Christ. That is how beautifully created you are. That is how much God loves you; He recreated you in His Son, the Beloved of God. Because of God's grace, you are now called the Beloved by Him. That is what it means to be His 'workmanship.'

For what end were we recreated, and made to be 'works of art'? Paul answers that question: *... for good works that God prepared beforehand, that we should walk in them.* We do not do the good works to be saved, we do the good works because we are saved. We are not supposed to be doing the good works to earn his favor, we already have that. His grace has already been given. Jesus came, died, and was resurrected. His blood has already been shed, and God's forgiveness has already been granted. The debt has already been paid. The account has already been settled, and the transaction has already taken place. The Law has already been fulfilled, and His wrath has already been appeased.

What I am saying to you is this: The work required for God's salvation has already been done by His grace, and is received through faith. There is no more work to earn His favor, because His favor has been granted to us by His grace. The only requirement to step into that great grace is faith. We must believe. That is our part. But that is the part the world has so much trouble with. Too many want to do the work. Too many want to take on the burden, do the job. "You gotta earn your way! No freeloaders allowed. You work for what you get." If we say that, we need to understand something. When we say we must keep ourselves saved, we are saying that Jesus was not enough. We make Him and His blood a common thing.

The Jews have to sacrifice every year for their sins, for every time they broke the Law. The blood of bulls and goats could only cover it. That blood was the common thing. The common animals could not save, it could only cover their sin. But Jesus is not common. Jesus' blood is not common. He was not an animal, whose blood could only cover sin. His blood was anything but common. His blood broke the chains that bound and shattered the yoke of 'earning your way.'

Our salvation does not rely on our good works, on our performance. It rests on His performance. It rests on what He accomplished. He attained our salvation for us. What is the proper mixture to attain salvation? God's great grace + our small measure of faith = an incredible and awesome salvation. Then, once we are saved, we become co-laborers *with* God, working the good works, not to be saved or to keep ourselves saved ... but because we are saved.

CHAPTER FIVE

The Weightier Matters …
Matter Most

IN THE PREVIOUS CHAPTER, we looked at the proper relationship, the proper mix, of works, faith, and grace. But what does the picture of that relationship look like? What does that reveal to others around us, both in and out of the Church body? Sadly, many of us can become so bound up with works-based salvation. Note that newly born-again Christians are especially susceptible to those chains. So many times, we feel that we need to perform to be accepted by God, and when that happens, God's tangible presence becomes removed from our daily lives. We become entrapped in this endless struggle of achieving His love, His mercy, and His grace. When our works become the source of our salvation instead of the evidence, we have chained ourselves to a life of misery, constantly seeking to perform, attain, and achieve His approval. It is that life of simply not accepting His grace, but rather working to earn it, that ultimately leads to failure and self-condemnation, both in ourselves and others around us. Instead of leaning into Him and His strength, we enter into a competition, constantly comparing our accomplishments both to other Christians and to ourselves. Our Christianity, our reliance on Him, then becomes more a show than a life. We become showmen instead of ministers, actors and actresses instead of sons and daughters of God. It is this showmanship that can be the downfall of so many, either by self-condemnation or pride.

Grace is not something we can achieve. It is not something we can perform and have it be paid to us because of that performance. Grace is not the wages of a job, or the earnings of a week's worth of work. Grace can never be considered something due us, because if it is payment due, it's no longer unmerited favor, but rather, a paycheck we have earned. Jesus reveals the true view of grace in the difference between two individuals in Luke Chapter 18.

(Luke 18:9-14) *Also He spoke this parable to some who trusted in themselves that they were righteous, and despised others: 'Two men went up to the temple to pray, one a Pharisee and the other a tax collector. The Pharisee stood and prayed thus with himself, God, I thank You that I am not like other men — extortioners, unjust, adulterers, or even as this tax collector. I fast twice a week; I give tithes of all that I possess.' And the tax collector, standing afar off, would not so much as raise his eyes to heaven, but beat his breast, saying, 'God, be merciful to me, a sinner!' I tell you, this man went down to his house justified rather than the other; for everyone who exalts himself will be humbled, and he who humbles himself will be exalted.*

Do you see the competition on the part of the Pharisee? Do you see the level of judgment and contempt towards the tax collector? The Pharisee was so focused on his own works, his own performance, that he missed the very definition of grace and what that grace offered him. This Pharisee listed the sins of everyone else while ignoring his own sins. How often do we, ourselves, turn a blind eye to God's grace while gazing in condemnation towards others? The Pharisee was so focused on how 'good' he was that he missed how full of grace God is.

The other man simply asked God to be merciful to him. No great list of grand works. No trophies to show for his incredible performances. No line of people singing his praises and writing down chronicles of his awesome accomplishments. He was just a man standing before a just God, asking for mercy. And what did Jesus say happened? It wasn't the Pharisee, who had kept receipt of all his good works that was justified. No, it was the man who clung to God's mercy. He is the one who was justified. It was the man who asked for grace, a favor that was not due him, who walked away justified.

But what about those who work for the approval of others? I mentioned how when we focus on works done for approval, our Christianity can become a show, and we become the showmen. What happens when life becomes only a show? William Shakespeare once wrote, "All the world's a stage, and all the men and women merely players ...." What a sad way of looking at life! But so many Christians have bound themselves spiritually to 'The Show.' They attempt to jump through the many hoops that religion has placed in front of them, doing what they can to be seen by those around them. They chase a false hope, displacing the real for the fake, the genuine for the phony. They become a spiritual Indiana Jones, but instead of taking the true gem—grace—they instead place the gem they already have onto the stone pedestal and grab hold of the useless bag of dirt. And then they become crushed under the weight of the stone trap set for them. Their 'form of godliness' is more important than the 'power thereof. '

Godliness is not an act. It is not the end result of an accomplishment. Godliness is not being a 'good person.' It is living a life of faith, trusting in Jesus and His sacrifice. In John Chapter 6, Jesus was asked by a crowd of people, "What must we be doing, to do the works of God?" Jesus' answer was very simple. In fact, there is a struggle with His answer in so many Christians today. Jesus did not say, "Heal the sick" or "Achieve a life without sin." He did not say, "Be perfect in the Law" or "Be only good, always." His answer: "This is the work of God that you believe in Him whom He has sent."

When we work for approval, either from God or man, we completely miss the awesome beauty of God's grace He has offered us. We become entangled in the cares of life that need not have any affect over us. We become trapped in the weeds of this world, and we become a fishing lure entangled in seaweed. We begin to become frayed as our connection to God becomes strained from the pressures of keeping up. Take a look at the two sisters of Lazarus in Luke 10:38-42.

(Luke 10:38-42) *Now it happened as they went that He entered a certain village; and a certain woman named Martha welcomed Him into her house. And she had a sister called Mary, who also sat at Jesus' feet and heard His word. But Martha was distracted with much serving, and she approached Him and said, "Lord, do You not care that my sister has left me to serve alone? Therefore tell her to help me." And Jesus answered and said to her, "Martha, Martha, you are worried and troubled about many things. But one thing is needed, and Mary has chosen that good part, which will not be taken away from her."*

Martha was busy. She was doing all the work 'and was distracted with much serving.' She wanted to make sure everything was just right, that everything that needed to be done (in her own eyes and understanding) was done. She even complained to Jesus about how much she was doing and how little her sister, Mary, was doing. She was working for Jesus' approval, and even accused Jesus of not caring about it at all. Meanwhile, Mary is sitting, she is resting at the feet of Jesus. What was Jesus' answer? While Martha is busy with working, there is one thing that was necessary. And Mary had chosen that one thing. To rest with Jesus. To sit at His feet and listen to His Word and find peace in His voice. Work will keep you busy, but busy work will keep you distracted from what is important: Jesus.

Too often distraction keeps us from realizing what is important. We can allow ourselves to become so focused with what we are doing that we miss the grace that surrounds us. If we are busy with busy work, then we will not see that others need the good fruit of God to be given to them.

Throughout Jesus' ministry, He constantly had issues with the Pharisees and how they thought God should be revealed. Jesus referred to them as a brood of vipers. He referred to them as whitewashed tombs, clean on the outside, but full of rotting bones on the inside. He referred to them as hypocrites and wicked. According to the Scriptures, Jesus felt strongly about what the Pharisees were. Why? They were the religious leaders of that time. They were the teachers of the Law and all that God had revealed. They were the ones you went to for answers to questions that were far above your paygrade. And Jesus had problems with them. In Matthew 23, Jesus really lays it all out for them, and He really doesn't hold much back. But I want to look at one particular verse in that chapter.

(Matthew 23:23) *Woe to you, scribes and Pharisees, hypocrites! For you pay tithe of mint and anise and cummin, and have neglected the weightier matters of the law: justice and mercy and faith. These you ought to have done, without leaving the others undone.*

The Pharisees were so focused on *keeping* the Law, even down to the smallest of details, that they pushed aside the revelation of God *in* the Law. Jesus said they 'neglected the weightier matters.' They pushed aside the revelation of God: justice, mercy, and faithfulness. Remember the two men we talked about earlier? The Pharisee and the tax collector? What did Jesus focus on there? Was it all the good works that the Pharisee had done? What about Mary and Martha? What did Jesus focus on? And what about Jesus speaking in the above verse? It is not about what they did, but how they lived.

We can keep the Law, and we can do all these good and great works, but if our hearts are not aligned right, we are missing the miracle of grace. God is not looking for the law-keepers, He already had One, and His name was Jesus. What he is looking for is a people who will walk with Him, who will be his people, and He will be their God. He is looking for people who will focus on the good portion he offers, instead of the good works they think He demands. A people who will allow themselves to be filled to overflowing with grace, and then pour out that grace onto any and all who are around them.

Micah 6:8 tells us exactly what God is looking for you to do: *To seek justice, to love mercy, and to walk humbly with your God.* Remember, with God, the weightier matters matter most.

CHAPTER SIX
But God ...

(**EPHESIANS 2:1-10**) *And you He made alive, who were dead in trespasses and sins, in which you once walked according to the course of this world, according to the prince of the power of the air, the spirit who now works in the sons of disobedience, among whom also we all once conducted ourselves in the lusts of our flesh, fulfilling the desires of the flesh and of the mind, and were by nature children of wrath, just as the others. But God, who is rich in mercy, because of His great love with which He loved us, even when we were dead in trespasses, made us alive together with Christ (by grace you have been saved), and raised us up together, and made us sit together in the heavenly places in Christ Jesus, that in the ages to come He might show the exceeding riches of His grace in His kindness toward us in Christ Jesus. For by grace you have been saved through faith, and that not of yourselves; it is the gift of God, not of works, lest anyone should boast. For we are His workmanship, created in Christ Jesus for good works, which God prepared beforehand that we should walk in them.*

We all have a past. We all have sinned, and we all have fallen short of God's glorious standard of holiness (see Romans 3:23). Every one of us has gone astray and walked away from the path of righteousness that God has set before us at one point or another, and many of us have rebelled to the point where we felt there was no return (see Isaiah 53:6).

Sin does so much more than simply bring shame; it kills. Sin destroys. Sin severed man from a trusting relationship with God and twisted that relationship from trust to fear. And we all were born with a sin nature. To sin was to be 'natural.'

We were destitute. We were dead in our trespasses. We were walking in our own understanding. We were following a slave master, driven by our own lusts and passions, seeking only our own fulfillment. Even the good we had done was swallowed up in pride and a sense of our own accomplishments. We were children of wrath, deserving the punishment of death. We were in need of a Savior.

The above passage from Ephesians Chapter 2 is one of my all-time favorite passages from the entire Bible. The Apostle Paul lays out the picture of God's grace so clearly and beautifully, the painting seems too good to be true. We had no ground to stand on, we were guilty of sin, and worthy of the death penalty that sin brings. "But God ..." You see, no matter where you come from, no matter where you have been, what you have done, what sins you have committed, no matter how guilty you are ... there is always, "But God ..."

(Isaiah 53:6) *All we like sheep have gone astray; We have turned, every one, to his own way; And the LORD has laid on Him the iniquity of us all.*

We have a past, yes ... but God has a new beginning. We have an old self, but God has a new creation. We have sinfulness, unrighteousness, and unholiness, but God has His sinlessness, His righteousness and His holiness. We have judgment, but God has justification. We have trespasses, but God has transformation. We have guilt, but God has forgiveness. We have sinful stains, but God has blood that washes us whiter than snow. We have everything that is wrong; He takes everything and makes it right. We have death, but God has life, and that life is more abundant!

Why did God save us? Why is there an Ephesians 2:4? Because God is rich in mercy. God is *wealthy*; He has an over-abundant supply of mercy. And because of that wealth of mercy, He loved us. He loved you, He loved me. Even when we were dead to Him in sin. Even when we were unreachable. Especially when we hated Him, reviled Him, and stood rebelliously against Him ... He loved us out of his abundance of mercy. There in Ephesians 2:4, Paul says that He had a "great love with which He loved us." In other words, I had sinned and needed a Savior; He loved and needed someone to save.

There is such a love for us from God, that even in our darkest, deepest, and most sin-filled times of our lives ... there was a 'but God.' And no matter where you are today, no matter how you feel today, no matter what you have done ... there is still Ephesians 2:4.

There is always Ephesians 2:4.

CHAPTER SEVEN
Jesus, the One Who is Willing

A STATEMENT I hear Christians say many times is: "Lord, are you willing to _______?" Or, "Lord, if it be Your will ..."

Many Christians have no problem with believing that God *can* do something, but the question they hold is: *will* God do what they have asked? I have often fallen into this way of thinking. We look at the majesty and power of God, and we have no doubt that God can heal us, deliver us, forgive us, and set us free. His power is far above anything we can ask or even think to ask, as the Apostle Paul wrote in Ephesians 3:20, *Now to Him who is able to do exceedingly abundantly above all that we ask or think, according to the power that works in us ...*

No, most Christians really don't have any problem holding faith in what God can do. But many times, our faith breaks down when we start talking about what God will do for us. In many ways, I believe it is an issue with our own humility. I know there are times I have this lofty idea of how to be humble. The picture is painted sometimes that to be humble, we must think, or feel, that we are beyond God's reach, that His grace cannot touch us. When we think that, and play that out in our prayer life, we let our misunderstanding of God's grace and mercy rob us of God's glory being revealed in us and through us.

We must, by the Holy Spirit, overcome those dangerous and disastrous thoughts. We must come to the realization that God not only can, but will, extend grace and mercy. But how do we do that? How do we overcome corrupt thinking? We must go to the Word of God, the Bible, and discover what He has already said. And then believe it. When we spend time diving into the Word, and take those moments to listen to His voice, our faith grows in acceptance of not only who He is, but what He will do for us.

Another area we sometimes struggle is understanding the Father Himself. We see Jesus' love and compassion. We see him heal the sick and deliver those in torment, pain, and suffering but when it comes to seeing the Father's will, we begin to struggle with the idea that the Father wants us healed and delivered. We see the grace of Christ, but sometimes, we have a hard time seeing the grace of the Father.

The Father is not holding out on us. He desires for us to walk in His grace and mercy. He desires for us to have His gifts, His love, and experience His compassion toward us. James writes in James 1:17-18, *Every good gift and every perfect gift is from above, and comes down from the Father of lights, with whom there is no variation or shadow of turning. Of His own will He brought us forth by the word of truth, that we might be a kind of first fruits of His creatures.*

Jesus also talked about the desire of God the Father to give to us His grace. In Matthew 7:7-11, Jesus says, *Ask, and it will be given to you; seek, and you will find; knock, and it will be opened to you. For everyone who asks receives, and he who seeks finds, and to him who knocks it will be opened. Or what man is there among you who, if his son asks for bread, will give him a stone? Or if he asks for a fish, will he give him a serpent? If you then, being evil, know how to give good gifts to your children, how much more will your Father who is in heaven give good things to those who ask Him!* So understand that what you see in Jesus, what you see Him do, you know that, too, is the Father's will.

In John 14, one of the disciples, Philip, asks Jesus to show them the Father, and that if He would, then that would be enough for them (the disciples). What was Jesus' answer? Jesus answers in John 14:9-10, *Have I been with you so long, and yet you have not known Me, Philip? He who has seen Me has seen the Father; so how can you say, 'Show us the Father'? Do you not believe that I am in the Father, and the Father in Me? The words that I speak to you I do not speak on My own authority; but the Father who dwells in Me does the works.*

What we see Jesus do and say, that is what the Father desires, does and says. So, what is it that we see Jesus ... do and say? In Mark 1:40-41, we read, *Now a leper came to Him, imploring Him, kneeling down to Him and saying to Him, 'If You are willing, You can make me clean.' Then Jesus, moved with compassion, stretched out His hand and touched him, and said to him, 'I am willing; be cleansed.'*

To Jesus, there was no question about His willingness. He answered simply, "I am willing." There are no times in Scripture that Jesus turned someone away. There are no times in Scripture where Jesus' answer to healing or deliverance was, "No, I am not willing." Even the Canaanite woman, who was outside the Covenant of God, was not turned away (see Matthew 15:21-28 and Mark 7:24-30).

We see this same attitude from Jesus throughout the Gospels. We see Him heal time and time again. We see Him give sight to the blind, we see Him forgive sins, we see Him raise the dead, and we even see Him doing such things on the Sabbath. We see Him confront the Pharisees and the Scribes, putting down their challenges all because He desires us to know the real God. He desires for us to experience the fullness of God's grace in our lives. We even see the Apostles heal and deliver in the Name of Jesus.

The ultimate show of God's grace toward us, and Jesus' willingness to do for us, is seen in Jesus going to the cross. We will be discussing that more in the next chapter, but let me just say this now: It was the Father's will that His Son should suffer and die for us on that old rugged cross. John 3:16 declares as much: *For God so loved the world that He gave His only begotten Son, that whoever believes in Him should not perish but have everlasting life.*

So we can rest in the understanding that God, in His great mercy and by his great grace, desires to heal us. We can rest knowing that Jesus and the Father are One, and that what you see Jesus do, you also see the Father do. We can stand on the rock of Jesus' statement: "I am willing." We no longer need to second-guess if Jesus will. Our faith can be full in knowing that not only can He, but also He will do what He has promised.

CHAPTER EIGHT

The Prodigal Son:

A Story of the Father's Grace,
a Sacrifice of Love … and Us.

(LUKE 15:11-24) *Then He said: A certain man had two sons. And the younger of them said to his father, 'Father, give me the portion of goods that falls to me.' So he divided to them his livelihood. And not many days after, the younger son gathered all together, journeyed to a far country, and there wasted his possessions with prodigal living. But when he had spent all, there arose a severe famine in that land, and he began to be in want. Then he went and joined himself to a citizen of that country, and he sent him into his fields to feed swine. And he would gladly have filled his stomach with the pods that the swine ate, and no one gave him anything.*

But when he came to himself, he said, 'How many of my father's hired servants have bread enough and to spare, and I perish with hunger! I will arise and go to my father, and will say to him, "Father, I have sinned against heaven and before you, and I am no longer worthy to be called your son. Make me like one of your hired servants."'

And he arose and came to his father. But when he was still a great way off, his father saw him and had compassion, and ran and fell on his neck and kissed him. And the son said to him, 'Father,

I have sinned against heaven and in your sight, and am no longer worthy to be called your son.'

But the father said to his servants, 'Bring out the best robe and put it on him, and put a ring on his hand and sandals on his feet. And bring the fatted calf here and kill it, and let us eat and be merry; for this my son was dead and is alive again; he was lost and is found.' And they began to be merry.

The Parable of the Prodigal Son is such a beautiful story of grace and a Father's love for his wayward, lost son. It is one of my favorite parables Jesus told. It is so full of God's grace and mercy to those of us who do not deserve it (read that as all of us!).

First, I want you to understand what the word 'prodigal' means. Prodigal simply means wasteful or riotous. In other words, a wasteful party of a life. The son takes his inheritance and goes far away and wastes it all on the party life. He is deeply lost in his own sin. He has made his bed, and now it is time to sleep in it. He reaches the lowest of the lowest points in his life when he realizes that even the pigs have better food than what he is eating, which is basically nothing. The Bible says he finally came to his senses. He then returns to his Father with a speech he has prepared. He is not just going back to his Father, but he is going to proclaim his sins to his Father, and he is expecting to be shunned at best. He is hoping he could find a place with the servants ... surely not as a cherished and loved son again.

That is the minefield of thinking that too many find themselves in. I know I have walked that minefield. They have taken all that has been given to them, the blessings, the securities, their very lives, and have wasted it all with their party living, a life of sin. They have fallen into the grip of sin, and are now entrapped in another world that has turned on them. Their only hope is to try to earn their way back into the good grace of their Father.

So here walks the son back home. But what is it that we see? Do we see a Father condemning his son? Do we see a Father with his nose upturned, refusing the son entrance into the home? Unfortunately, that is what so many have been told and now believe about God. They've been told that God is finished with them, or that He barely has enough forgiveness for them because their sins are too great for even God to forgive and forget. Sure, you can return, but you are going to have to pay for what you have done …

We don't see any of that from the Father in this parable. Instead, what we do see is the exact opposite. We see a Father who is watching for the son's return. And when he sees him from afar, the Father throws all resemblance of dignity to the side and rushes to meet the returning son. He *rushes* to his son! The Bible says the Father ran to the son and fell on his neck and kissed him! The Father only had eyes for the return of the son!

The son, to his credit, through what is surely shock and confusion, begins his prepared speech. But the Father doesn't even seem to hear him, and not only that, he interrupts him. In verse 22, the Father tells the servants to go and bring the best robe, and to put a ring on the son's hand and sandals on his feet. He then says something very interesting. He tells them to go and get the fatted calf and to kill it, because there is going to be some merry-making going on! They are going to *party*!

You see, the picture Jesus paints here of a Father meeting with his wayward, lost, wasteful living son is not one of condemnation. It is not one full of glares of contempt, anger, and judgment. It is one of compassion. It is one that reveals a Father who is watching for the son to return, waiting for the son to finally 'come to his senses.'

Our return to God after moments of sin, or perhaps a lifetime of it, is often done like the son expected here. We return to God, not expecting Him to love us, not really. Sure, He might forgive us, but probably not, and surely He will never forget the horrible things we have done. We will have to face those things every day for the rest of our miserable lives. After all, how could someone, especially a holy and just God, love me after what I have done? What else could I be but unlovable? What else have I done but the unforgivable, and definitely the unforgettable? But this picture that Jesus reveals of the Father is not what we have been told and taught. The Father that Jesus reveals to us is full of mercy, grace, and love. He is full of compassion, forgiveness, and yes, even forgetfulness.

This Father God we have? He watched for us, and He watches for those still lost. He ran to us, fell on our necks and rained down on us with kisses. And He desires every other one who is lost to return, because He watches for them also, and He will run to meet them when He sees them, and He will lavish upon them the kisses from a loving, caring, and very personal Father God.

The grace message of the Father is incredible in this story of the Prodigal Son. There is another character tucked away in the text, but still so clear and obvious. A character I never noticed before rereading this story to teach in the Kids Ministry at our church one week. Who is this unnoticed character? In verse 23, we read of him: *And bring the fatted calf here and kill it, and let us eat and be merry ...* How many times have I read over this passage, thought about this story, and never really paid much attention to the 'fatted calf'?

The Father did not ignore the wayward son's sin. The

Father dealt with it; it just wasn't in the expected and predictable form of punishment to the son. There was nothing the son could ever really do to 'earn back' all that he wasted in his living in sin. The son knew that, which is why he had his big speech prepared. The Father knew that, which is why He showed compassion on the son. But there still had to be blood shed to cover sin. The Bible tells us in Hebrews 9:22, *And according to the law almost all things are purified with blood, and without shedding of blood there is no remission.* This echoes Leviticus 17:11, which reads, *For the life of the flesh is in the blood, and I have given it to you upon the altar to make atonement for your souls; for it is the blood that makes atonement for the soul.*

How did The Father deal with the sin problem? There was a sacrifice. There was the shedding of blood. The word translated 'kill' in Luke 15:23 is not the same word used for murder or even to kill an animal for a meal. It was the word used for sacrifice, to slay the paschal lamb. The Father offered up the best He had to offer: the healthiest, the best ... the fatted calf. This fatted calf is a picture of none other than Christ, Himself. He was the Lamb of God, slain before the foundations of the world. He was the sacrifice offered up for the sins of the world. How could I have read this passage so many times over the years and not see Jesus in the story?

John 3:16 tells us, *For God so loved the world that He gave His only begotten Son, that whoever believes in Him should not perish but have everlasting life.* It is easy to see God's love in this passage. But there is another side to this verse. There are two parts to this grace of God: (1) God so loved that He gave His only begotten Son, and (2) The Son so loved that He allowed Himself to be given.

In the parable of the Prodigal Son, we have the wayward,

lost, sinful, and pitiful son. We also have the ever watchful, full of grace and mercy Father. But we also see the One who gave up all He had, in fact His very life, for the sins of the lost son: Jesus represents the fatted calf. The Parable of the Prodigal Son is truly one of the greatest stories of love, mercy, and grace. It is a story of a Father's grace, a sacrifice, and us.

CHAPTER NINE
This Jesus

(LUKE 23:39-43) *Then one of the criminals who were hanged blasphemed Him, saying, "If You are the Christ, save Yourself and us." But the other, answering, rebuked him, saying, "Do you not even fear God, seeing you are under the same condemnation? And we indeed justly, for we receive the due reward of our deeds; but this Man has done nothing wrong." Then he said to Jesus, "Lord, remember me when You come into Your kingdom." And Jesus said to him, "Assuredly, I say to you, today you will be with Me in Paradise."*

Throughout this book, we have looked at God's amazing grace towards us, and what that truly means. We have seen in the Scripture His incredible love for us and the cost He willingly paid to bring us into a right relationship with Him. That cost was nothing short of the death of His Son, Jesus. The Scripture also shows us that the Son willingly paid the ultimate price in laying down His own precious life for us. But with all of God's grace, all of His love and mercy, we all must come to the point of a decision, a decision that we alone can make.

You see, this Jesus was more than a mere man. He was the Christ, the Son of the Living God. He was the great I AM. He was both God and Man, truly, Immanuel, God with us. He left the richness of heaven to come to this earth, to live as we live, to breathe as we breathe, and to walk as we walk. He took on flesh, living a perfect life. Human blood flowed through His veins. He felt the dirt in the desert, and He experienced the harshness of the land. And on the cross, He died. There was finality in that statement of fact. The Christ, the One promised, the One whom hope hung upon ... died. And not just died, but died a brutal, painful, and tormenting death.

But in dying, He revealed His true purpose. With His blood shed, He gave Himself as a sacrifice. His life of sinlessness was given for the lives of sinners. Sinners who were spiritually dead and pitiful creatures, lost in their own sinfulness and sworn enemies of the One who truly loved them. What, exactly, was His purpose? To set right the wrong, to set free the slave, and to let loose the captive. He came into this world to save the sinner, to seek those who were lost. That was me ... and that was you.

We all were in need of a Savior. The Bible tells us in Isaiah 53, *All we like sheep have gone astray; We have turned, every one, to his own way.* We all have followed our own path, our own righteousness, and our own wisdom. And we all have suffered for those decisions. We all have faced mountains that we ourselves built with our own hands of clay. We all faced a death penalty we could not pay, a sentence we could not endure. But just when the night seemed to be at its darkest, there was a gleaming, bright shining light on the horizon. The Savior had come! Our debt had been paid, and our lives were no longer forfeit! Christ had come to ransom you, and He had come to ransom me! Could this be true? Could this Man, this Jesus, truly love us so much that His life was given on that old rugged cross, and His blood was poured out on that dry, dirty ground for us!?

Truly, yes it was. But where do we go from there? We see this Jesus on the cross, and the Bible says that He did not even appear as a man. He was wounded, He was stricken, He was chastised, He was despised, He was spit on, He was brutalized. He was killed. And killed for whom? You. Me. Us. And so, again, where do we go from there? Where do we go from the beatings He endured? Where do we go from His humiliation? We were the transgressors, not Him. And yet, there He was, on the cross, dying. Yes, where do we go from there?

In this chapter's opening passage of Scripture, we read of a brief conversation between Jesus and the two thieves hanging on their own crosses on either side of Him. There was Jesus hanging between the two men. What do we see? This scene has been painted, sculpted, and shown in so many ways and places over the years. I have seen this picture so many times, I can not count the number. And so in Luke, we get a very interesting look at this picture.

There are two thieves. Two different men, but both dying for the same crimes. The Bible tells us that the wages of sin is death (Romans 6:23). There is a death penalty to the one who commits sin, and it is a death penalty that must be paid. Both thieves are there, dying for the crimes they committed. In Luke, we see that one of the criminals challenges Jesus, even going so far as blaspheming Him. *If you are the Christ, save Yourself and us.*

How many today shout that same challenge at Him? "If you truly are Christ, get me out of this mess I brought myself into!" The audacity! The ignorant boasting of a dying man to make demands! But I wonder, how many times have I said the same thing? How about you? How many times has your back been up against the wall and those words came flowing out of your mouth? "If you are God …"

We then see the other criminal speak up. He asks the challenging criminal a question: *"Do you not even fear God, seeing you are under the same condemnation?"* He goes on, *"We indeed do receive this same condemnation justly, for we receive due reward for our deeds; but this man has done nothing wrong."* The man then says to Jesus, *"Lord, remember me when You come into Your kingdom."*

What's the difference between the two criminals? They both committed the same crimes, as they were both thieves. They both were given the same death sentence, as they were both being crucified. The difference between the two meant the difference in eternity. One cursed Jesus, blasphemed Him, and demanded salvation, though temporary it would have been ("... save Yourself and us"). The other admitted his guilt, and truly repented. He reconsidered 'this man,' and this criminal asked to be remembered when Jesus entered into His kingdom. And that man was rewarded by This Man with the words of the crucified Christ: "Assuredly, I say to you, today you will be with Me in Paradise."

The picture in this passage reveals us before Christ. You are at the crossroads, the cross, and what will your decision be? The evidence of God's grace is laid out before you, but what will you do with it? What will you do with this Jesus? You can curse God, blaspheme His Name, and reject the grace offered. Or you can recognize who He is, what He accomplished at the cross, and cry out to Him and receive His grace into your own life, becoming a born again, child of God. But the decision is ultimately yours: What will you do with this Jesus?

Meet the Author

CHRIS BELLER lives in Michigan with his wife of twenty-two years, Stephanie, and their three children, Christian, Jacob, and Azaria. He enjoys studying the Bible, teaching and preaching the Gospel of Jesus Christ, playing and collecting board games, and fishing.